SEVENOAKS & AROUND

THROUGH TIME

Russell Harper

AMBERLEY PUBLISHING

First published 2013

Amberley Publishing
The Hill, Stroud, Gloucestershire, GL5 4EP
www.amberley-books.com

Copyright © Russell Harper, 2013

The right of Russell Harper to be identified as the
Author of this work has been asserted in accordance with
the Copyrights, Designs and Patents Act 1988.

ISBN 978 1 4456 1837 1 (print)
ISBN 978 1 4456 1844 9 (ebook)

British Library Cataloguing in Publication Data.
A catalogue record for this book is available from the
British Library.

Typesetting by Amberley Publishing.
Printed in Great Britain.

Introduction

'Sevenoaks? Don't you mean One Oak?!'

If it wasn't well-known before, the hurricane of October 1987 really put the Kent town of Sevenoaks on the map. The town's position on the Greensand ridge above the Kentish Weald left it exposed to the full force of the storm. More than half the trees in the 1,000-acre Knole Park were felled, but it was the sight of six of the seven oak trees on The Vine cricket ground blown over that captured the public's imagination.

In fact, these seven trees were not the original ones that gave the town its name. In an old register book at Rochester, written around 1115, there is a list of churches in the diocese, and among them is *Seouanaca*, the Anglo-Saxon for Sevenoaks. It is not known for certain where the seven oaks of Saxon times stood, but the town has always sought to live up to its motto, *Floreant Septum Quercus*: 'May the Seven Oaks Flourish', and groups of seven oak trees have been planted on the Tonbridge road near the White Hart and at Raley's Field, as well as on The Vine, where they were restored to their full complement after the hurricane.

Sevenoaks has steadily grown from its Saxon origins. Its location between London and the South Coast made it a convenient stop-off point for travellers and traders, with a market being established early on. In 1456 the then Archbishop of Canterbury bought the Knole estate (for £266!) and built Knole House, which is today a jewel in the crown of both Sevenoaks and the National Trust, owning the house and part of Knole Park. Other estates were established in and around the town. These were bought by wealthy individuals, such as Ralph Bosville, gentleman of Lincoln's Inn, who bought the Bradbourne estate in 1555, and Thomas Farnaby, who bought Kippington in 1630, making his money from teaching the sons of the nobility. They are now remembered in street names, such as Bosville Drive and Farnaby Drive.

In the 1860s, the railway came to the area, first to Bat and Ball and later to Sevenoaks at Tubs Hill, transforming the town. Being able to travel daily from Sevenoaks to London made the town attractive to a new generation of commuters. Suburban villas sprang up near the stations, and shops and schools increased in number to support these new households.

The Sevenoaks landscape changed further in the years after the First World War, which had claimed the lives of so many men, both from the families of the large households and from their staff. Many of these large households soon became unviable, and many estates were sold off, freeing land for new housing. Among the houses that fell victim to this particular wind of change were Bradbourne House, which was sold in 1927, and Chipstead Place and Montreal, which were both demolished in the 1930s. Houses now occupy what had been rolling pasture and formal gardens in the years gone by.

Around two-thirds of the images in this book are of Sevenoaks itself, the rest covering the surrounding villages of Riverhead, Dunton Green, Otford, Seal, Kemsing, Chipstead, Sevenoaks Weald, and Underriver. These show that some areas, such as Tubs Hill and the centre of Riverhead, have changed enormously over the last hundred years or so, while others, such as the Upper High Street and centre of the village of Otford, have altered very little.

The Sevenoaks Society is an association of local people who care about the character and appearance of the town and its surroundings, and who have a particular interest in preserving and improving Sevenoaks for both current and future generations. Information about the society and how to join can be found at www.sevenoakssociety.org.uk. If anyone would like more information about the area than I have been able to provide in this visual guide, I would strongly recommend *Sevenoaks, An Historical Dictionary* by David Killingray and Elizabeth Purves (2012).

The Seven Oaks, Tonbridge Road, Sevenoaks.

The Seven Oaks

Although not the original seven trees that were believed to have given the town its name, these seven oak trees stood on Tonbridge Road from the eighteenth century until they were felled in 1954 (*inset*). Although believed at the time to have been diseased, they were in fact found to have been healthy. The oaks that now stand here were planted in 1955.

The White Hart, *c.* 1905

The White Hart was established in the early seventeenth century and thrived as a coaching inn, serving travellers seeking refreshment on what was a two-day journey by stagecoach from London to the South Coast. The stables area shown to the left of the pub subsequently made way for a car dealership, but more recently a small housing development was built on this part of the site.

The Upper High Street, 1920s

This part of the town has changed very little over the years, and at first glance the only obvious difference between the two views is the cars. In fact, the terrace of four late eighteenth-century cottages to the centre left of the old image is now a terrace of three. The cottage to the left of the original terrace had to be demolished for the widening of Oak Lane to accommodate increasing twentieth-century traffic.

Raley's Corner, 1860s

Raley's Corner was named after a baker and pastry cook who once traded here. Like the Upper High Street, the buildings here have changed little over the years, the building on the far left being the only casualty, having been replaced by Temple House in 1884. The road here often feels rather narrow for twenty-first-century traffic.

The Upper High Street, 1940s

The impressive-looking building to the right was The White House. Formerly two cottages, possibly dating from Tudor times, it was rebuilt in the early nineteenth century, when the imposing façade was added. It was antique dealers' premises for many years. Although Grade II listed, in 1963 the owner of the building applied for permission to demolish it, and after a lengthy battle it was finally taken down in the early 1970s.

The High Street & London Road, *c.* 1900
The tile-hung building on the left is called the Bishop's House, having been built in the fifteenth century when it was the principal residence of the Reeve of the Archbishop of Canterbury. Although it is now a fish restaurant (Loch Fyne), many will still remember it as Outram's, which opened in 1880 as a saddler's, and later sold sports and travel goods before closing in 2001.

Sevenoaks Coffee Tavern and Fountain, *c.* 1900

If you thought that coffee shops were a fairly recent introduction to the town, you may be surprised to learn that the Sevenoaks Coffee Tavern opened at the junction of the High Street and London Road in 1886. The building later became a restaurant and then a dairy. The HSBC Bank now occupies the site. The fountain was a gift from an anonymous benefactor in 1882.

Sevenoaks Market Place, *c.* 1910

The market has been a part of Sevenoaks life for hundreds of years, and markets have been held where the High Street meets London Road since the thirteenth century. This early twentieth-century view shows cattle pens outside The Chequers pub, although the livestock market here was in fact in decline at this time. A food market is now held here every Wednesday and Saturday, under the management of Sevenoaks Town Council.

The Market Place Looking South, *c.* 1870
It's many years since playing cricket in the High Street was an option for the children of Sevenoaks, but in the late nineteenth century the greatest danger might have been from an irate shopkeeper unlucky enough to have a ball hit through his window.

High Street Shops, c. 1980

Kent's opened on the site of what had been the town's main post office, which had moved to its present South Park corner location in 1970. To the right of Kent's are the offices of the *Sevenoaks Chronicle*, which were rebuilt when Waitrose moved to this site in 1983. The newspaper's offices are now in the Sevenoaks Business Centre. The Waitrose building has recently been rebuilt, bringing with it something new to the town: an escalator.

Redman's Place, c. 1900

Redman's place is now little more than an alleyway running from the High Street down the side of Lorimers to the rear entrance of Waitrose, but the 1891 census records that there were sixteen terraced houses here, all taking their water from a well and pump in the yard. The houses were demolished as part of a slum clearance in 1961.

High Street Shops, *c.* 1900

At the centre of the picture is Marchant and Wright's, the draper's, now the Halifax Building Society. To the right is the Rose and Crown, a coaching inn popular with market traders and visitors. It closed its doors in 1936, was demolished, and rebuilt as Young's department store in 1938. It is now M&Co.

The Oddfellows & Foresters Arms, *c.* 1950
Of all the pubs that have served the town's residents and visitors, this must have been the smallest. It opened in 1891 and closed in 1955, becoming a wine merchant's and then a charity shop. It has been the Mobile Phone Centre since the late 1990s.

No. 101 High Street, *c.* 1880 & *c.* 1930

No. 101 High Street, 1989 & 2013
This important Grade II listed seventeenth-century building occupies a prominent position on the corner of the High Street and Dorset Street. It is recorded as having been a sweetshop in 1859, then had a number of different owners until 1982 when it was left empty and fell into a state of disrepair. Renovated in 1989, it has been an estate agent's since that time.

Bank Street, 1860s

When this photograph was taken, the Methodist chapel will have only recently been built. It was built in local ragstone as part of a group of buildings, comprising of the chapel itself, a school, and accommodation for ministers and teachers. The buildings did not serve their original purpose for long, as shops had been inserted into the former school hall by 1903, around the time a new Methodist church and halls were opened in The Drive. Many of the shops in Bank Street were built as houses.

'The Grey House', No. 120 High Street, c. 1950s

This was an early to mid-nineteenth-century building, which was rendered around 1900. Until 1938, it was for many years Parris's café, and then became Timothy White's, shown here. It was knocked down and replaced with a branch of Boots in the early 1970s, following Boots' takeover of Timothy White's.

High Street, *c.* 1860

The building on the left is a farrier's forge (note the hitching post outside). This is now Hoad's shoe shop. Hoad's was established in Sevenoaks in 1898. It now has a separate children's shoe shop in London Road. To its right is the Holmesdale Tavern, which boasted five bars. On the far right is Bligh's Hotel and brewery. Bligh's (now The Oak Tree) is the only one of these buildings to have survived.

Hoad's Shoe Shop, 1946

As well as many national chains, Sevenoak's shopping streets have retained a number of long-established local businesses. Horncastles was established in 1888 and Lorimers in 1920. Shoe retailer C. F. Hoad & Sons Ltd was established in the town in 1898. Cousins John and James (seen here serving a customer just as his predecessors did) are the fourth generation of the Hoad family to manage the business, which now also has branches in Wandsworth and Deal, as well as a seperate children's shop in London Road, Sevenoaks.

High Street Entrance to Brewery Lane, *c.* 1920
In the mid-nineteenth century there were two breweries in the High Street. This is the entrance to the Holmesdale Brewery next to Bethlehem Farm, which was bought by John Bligh in 1862. He sold the brewery to Watney Coombe Reid in 1911 and it closed in 1935.

Bethlehem Farm, c. 1900

Originally dating from the sixteenth century, this farmhouse was rented by the Bethlehem Hospital for the Insane, but was renamed Bligh's when bought by John Bligh in 1882. He turned the farmhouse into a hotel, and then bought the adjoining brewery and the nearby Holmesdale Tavern. John became a very successful businessman. At one point he owned some twenty-seven public houses in and around the town. Still often referred to as Bligh's, the pub is now called The Oak Tree.

Entrance to Bethlehem Farm, *c.* 1875
These farm buildings stood between Bligh's and Pembroke Road; the entrance shown here now leads into the Bligh's shopping centre car park. The two oast houses faced onto Pembroke Road. By 1919, these buildings had become derelict and were pulled down, with the land being sold.

Suffolk Place, *c.* 1901
This terrace at the north end of the High Street was originally built as private houses, which they remained for almost a hundred years before being converted into shops in 1936/37. The original residents were professional people such as doctors and dentists.

The Granada Cinema, *c.* 1950

The Granada was at one time one of four cinemas in Sevenoaks. Opened as The Cinema in November 1935, it replaced an earlier purpose-built cinema on the same site, and could accommodate 1,200 people. It was renamed The Plaza in 1937 and The Granada in 1948. It closed in October 1960, and the site was cleared and became the entrance of Suffolk Way.

Smith's Brewery, *c.* 1880

The brewery was established on the High Street, at what is now the entrance to Suffolk Way, in 1830. Alfred Smith and his son Percy owned and ran the business from 1880, and by 1900 they controlled twenty-three pubs in the Sevenoaks district. Percy Smith sold the business in 1899 and brewing then ended on the site. One of the brewery buildings was subsequently converted into an electric cinema, the first in the town.

Bethlehem Farm Oast Houses, *c.* 1860

These oasts were part of the Bethlehem Farm brewery, and faced onto Pembroke Road. Demolished almost 100 years ago, there is a clue to their presence in the name of the flats above the shops at this end of the High Street: Oastfield Court.

Manor Cottages, *c.* 1935

Like other properties in the town centre, the shops on this site, on the northern corner of Pembroke Road and the High Street, started life as private homes. In this case, the house on the far right-hand side of the terrace remains (it is currently a nail bar). The rest were redeveloped into the shops we see today, which include the ever-popular Sevenoaks Bookshop.

Royal Crown Hotel, *c.* 1900

An inn since 1622, when rebuilt in the mid-nineteenth century, the Royal Crown became the epicentre of the Sevenoaks social scene. With its luxury bars and large ballroom, the hotel hosted all sorts of events, from dinners, dances and grand balls to auctions and meetings.

Royal Crown Hotel, *c.* 1900

The Royal Crown was demolished in the 1930s, some years after the hotel had been closed. The Majestic cinema was built on part of the site in 1937 and the present post office in 1970.

Royal Crown Hotel Gardens, *c.* 1900
The Royal Crown stood in 12 acres of gardens, which included a vegetable garden, a miniature farm that helped to stock the hotel kitchens, and an aviary.

The Odeon Cinema,
c. 1970
Built as The Majestic
in 1937 on the site
of the Royal Crown
Hotel, this purpose-
built cinema, later
renamed The Odeon,
became the fourth in
the town. Although
now often referred to
as The Stag Theatre,
the theatre didn't open
until 1983, following
a long campaign by
the Sevenoaks Theatre
Action Group (STAG)
to bring a theatre to
the town, and a year
and a half of internal
remodelling. Now called
the Stag Community Arts
Centre, it houses a large
sound stage and two
digital cinemas, as well
as other performance and
meeting facilities.

Post Office & Telephone Exchange, South Park, *c.* 1920

The original Sevenoaks post office was in the High Street (where Waitrose now stands) but moved to South Park in 1897, on the opposite side of the road to the current post office.

London Road Entrance to the Shambles, *c.* 1865

The Shambles, the area of alleyways and courtyards between the High Street and London Road, are the oldest part of the town, dating from the mid-fifteenth century. The area was mainly used by the meat trade, as depicted in the murals added in 1999. The shop to the right of the picture, now Knole House Furnishings, was the site of the old town jail. The Swan pub on the left later became the Dorset Arms, but is now a restaurant.

Lime Tree Walk

Lime Tree Walk was the work of the renowned architect Thomas Jackson. Built in 1878/79 it was a development of twenty-four cottages for local workers, and the Lime Tree Temperance Hotel. The houses originally had views across the hotel's tennis courts and croquet lawn. Modern flats now occupy that land.

The Lime Tree Hotel, 1900s

The Lime Tree Temperance Hotel was built in Lime Tree Walk in 1880. Guests had to sign a pledge of teetotalism, but, although worthy, this seems to have been a less than successful business strategy and the name eventually changed to the Lime Tree Hotel. It closed in the 1930s and the *Sevenoaks News* moved in. It has been The Sevenoaks Business Centre since 1996. The *Sevenoaks Chronicle* offices moved here in 2012.

London Road, *c.* 1905

The sight of a photographer, with his large, heavy camera, could still draw quite a crowd in the early years of the twentieth century. The photographer in this case is likely to have been Charles Essenheigh Corke, who took a number of the early photographs in this book, whose studio can be seen at the far right of the photograph. The site is now Zizzi's.

Caslake Coachbuilders, c. 1860

This building pre-dates the arrival of the motor car by some years, Caslake specialising in the building and maintenance of horse-drawn transport. The pillars at the front of the building were spaced widely enough for carriages to pass in and out. Hely & Co. took over the business in 1880, and began selling and servicing early motor cars from 1901. Today, the ground floor of the building is home to print and design company Ditto.

London Road Looking South, *c.* 1900

The ivy-clad building shown here was built in the early eighteenth century as the Sevenoaks Savings Bank. Among those who have occupied the building are the Sevenoaks and District Scouts and *Sevenoaks News*. It was then an auction house for some years and is now a restaurant. The building is Grade II listed. The building on the right was at this time the offices of the Sevenoaks Division of the Liberal Association.

London Road Looking North, 1860s

When this photograph was taken the road surface was still compacted earth, which was difficult to negotiate with horse-drawn vehicles. The railings on the left are for St Nicholas' Infant School. At the bottom of the hill the large walnut tree at the site of the Arboretum is visible, which had a public water pump outside. It was a private house, then offices and later a café. Empty from 1968, it was pulled down in 1973.

High Street and the Constitutional Club, *c.* 1900

To the right of the modern photograph (2008) is what had been Ideas, a DIY store, boarded up, and Edwards Electricals that was to close soon afterwards. The building, which had originally been a garage and car dealership, was pulled down, and at the time of writing the site remains empty and something of an eyesore.

Constitutional Club, *c.* 1905
This impressive red-brick building was built in 1889 for Conservative social and political meetings. To the rear was the Club Hall, which held concerts and meetings and could seat 500 people. The Club Hall was destroyed by a bomb in the Second World War. The club itself closed in 1957, and the building was converted to apartments in the 1990s.

51564. SEVENOAKS. THE VINE RECREATION GROUND

The Vine Recreation Ground, *c.* 1905

The brick wall in the early photograph is the rear of the Club Hall. Following its destruction in the Second World War, the Vine Gardens were laid out, with flower beds and a fish pond with a wooden bridge over. The nursery glasshouses on the right became the site of a car dealership, and the site is now a small development of luxury homes.

The Vine Recreation Ground, *c.* 1905

The Sevenoaks Town Band formed in 1890, and wealthy local businessman Henry Swaffield paid for a bandstand to be built here in 1894. In 1902, he also paid for the neighbouring band practice room. The band disbanded in the 1990s but the bandstand is still used from time to time. The Sevenoaks and Tonbridge Concert Band played there during the Town Council's celebration of the Queen's Diamond Jubilee in 2012.

The Vine, c. 1910
This view of The Vine gives a clear view of the Vine Tavern, now the Vine Restaurant, these days obscured by trees. The war memorial commemorates 226 Sevenoaks residents who lost their lives in the First World War, and a further 115 from the Second World War.

The Vine, *c.* 1905
Not a common sight in the town these days, here a farmer who has attended the livestock market shepherds his herd of cows in the direction of St Botolph's Road. Behind them, the Constitutional Club and Club Hall are visible.

Dartford Road Shops, *c.* 1905
The land around what is now Vine Court Road and Avenue Road was developed in the late nineteenth century following the demolition of Vine Court itself. The new houses were built to meet the demand of professional families for properties within close proximity of the new railway station at Tubs Hill. These shops (which included Lorimer's, now located in the High Street) opened to cater for these new arrivals.

Upper St. John's, Sevenoaks

Dartford Road Shops, *c.* 1905

Dartford Road, along with London Road, is one of the oldest roads in Sevenoaks, used from Medieval times to take livestock from the North Downs to the weald. Like those at the Vine end of Dartford Road, the shops here on the corner of Hollybush Lane grew to serve the growing population in this area after the arrival of the railway. This area retains a village feel and has enjoyed something of a renaissance in recent years, with the arrival of Rafferty's Café and a number of individual shops.

London Road, Kelly and Fletcher Car Dealership, 1960s

Formerly the site of a Vauxhall and Jaguar dealership, this site was redeveloped in recent years and is now home to the prestige dealerships Bentley Kent and Lamborghini Sevenoaks.

The Rock and Fountain, London Road, 1900s
One of the town's many lost pubs, The Rock and Fountain at No. 139 London Road offered cheap accommodation for travellers. It closed in 1959 and subsequently became a car dealership. Until recently it was a second-hand furniture market, but it is currently vacant.

Sevenoaks District Council Offices, 1970s

The Arboretum (*inset*), also known as the Pump House and Walnut Tree House, occupied the piece of land in the middle of this picture until 1973. Behind are the old offices of Sevenoaks District Council in Argyle Road. The council offices were redeveloped in 1985, and new premises built on the corner of Argyle Road and Eardley Road where the public baths were originally situated. The building in the foreground of the scene today belongs to West Kent Housing Association, and the council offices are behind it.

Tubs Hill, Early 1960s

By the early 1960s, most of the houses and shops on the west side of Tubs Hill had been earmarked for redevelopment, and they are shown here ready for demolition. Two large office blocks were built here in 1964, with further development having taken place since. One of the office blocks of Tubs Hill House is now going to be converted into a hotel.

Lower Tubs Hill, *c.* **1961**
The private homes in this lower part of Tubs Hill were demolished to make way for Tubs Hill Parade, a row of shops with flats above and car parking for shoppers.

Station Cinema, 1930s
One of the town's four cinemas, this cinema opened in 1912 as the Palace Theatre and was later variously known as the Elite Palace, the Cinema Theatre and the Sevenoaks Cinema before becoming a cycle and motorcycle garage and then a branch of Lloyds Bank.

Sevenoaks Tubs Hill, Station Approach, c. 1900
What is now the town's main railway station was actually the second to open. Bat and Ball station opened in 1862 and Sevenoaks (originally Sevenoaks Tubs Hill) in 1868. To the left of the photograph is the Railway and Bicycle pub, which was demolished in 2008 to make way for flats.

Station Parade. Sevenoaks 6639

Sevenoaks Tubs Hill Station & The Sennocke Hotel, 1930s

The other pub at Sevenoaks station was The Farmers (opened in 1868 as the Sennocke Hotel), which was popular with those attending the market opposite the pub in Hitchen Hatch Lane as well as rail travellers. It remained popular into the twenty-first century. Despite a campaign to save it from closure, the trust that owned the freehold of the land sold the site and the pub was pulled down in 2006. At the time of writing the site is still awaiting development.

Tubs Hill Station, 1967

The opening of the railway station by the South Eastern and Chatham Railway on 2 March 1868, providing fast services to London, was a major factor in the growth and rising prosperity of Sevenoaks. This photograph shows the original station building, which was adjacent to the platforms (at the site of the photograph inset). The old buildings were demolished in 1977 and replaced with a new building, which is shown here following updating work in 2012.

Tubs Hill Station, *c.* 1900

The redevelopment of the station in the 1970s took away the platforms seen at either side of this picture. There were two serious rail crashes here. In 1884, two trains collided at the station and the two crew of one of them were both killed. In 1927, a locomotive derailed between Sevenoaks and Dunton Green, killing thirteen people and injuring twenty.

The Halfway House, London Road, *c.* 1905

Of the three pubs in the immediate vicinity of the railway station (the others being The Farmers and the Railway and Bicycle), this is the only survivor. The Halfway House is an independent pub. The building's nineteenth-century frontage hides a much older building behind.

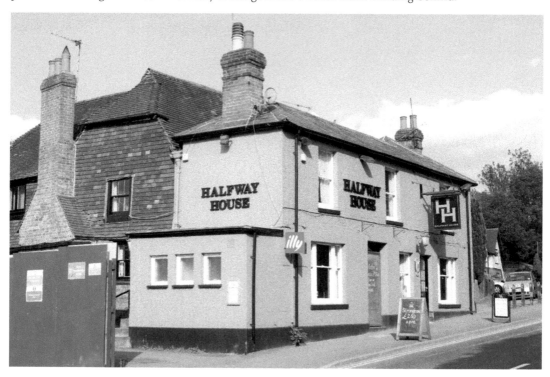

The Bluebird Garage, 1950s

Next door to the Halfway House was the Bluebird garage and Morewood's timber yard. Until recently it was a car dealership, but the area has now been cleared for the construction of a branch of the low-cost retailer Lidl, the news of which caused some controversy.

Quakers Hall Lane, Sevenoaks.

Quakers Hall Lane, 1920s

There have been Quakers in Sevenoaks since the 1650s, and their Meeting House is in Hollybush Lane. The church of St John the Baptist is out of shot to the left. The building on the right is the original St John's Church of England Primary School, which was demolished in the 1970s. The school moved to Bayham Road, into what had been Bayham Road Boys' School.

Upper St John's Hill, *c.* 1900

Until the mid-nineteenth century St John's Hill was often referred to as Workhouse Hill, after the workhouse at the junction with Camden Road. These buildings have changed relatively little since this photograph was taken. The main addition to the scene now is the St John's Hill Surgery building, which occupies what was a garden on the corner of Camden Road.

St John's Hill, *c.* 1905

The early photograph shows a neat and apparently thriving parade of shops near to Sevenoaks Hospital. Nowadays, it is a rather less attractive scene. Although a new pizza restaurant has recently opened here, the two shops closest to the camera have been boarded up for a number of years. At the time of writing, The Castle pub is up for sale.

Sevenoaks Hospital, 1927

The late nineteenth-century growth of the town created a need for hospital facilities, and the Holmesdale Cottage Hospital opened in 1873. Initially comprised of just eight beds and one nurse, the hospital was expanded a number of times over the years. The hospital now provides outpatient facilities. It has a busy a Minor Injuries Unit equipped with X-ray facilities, and it has a hydrotherapy pool.

Wells' Cycle Shop, St John's Hill, 1900s

Cycling became enormously popular during Victorian times. By 1912 there were at least four cycle shops in the centre of the town, and the Lime Tree Hotel became the main meeting place for cyclists. Mr Wells's son H. G. Wells (named after the science fiction writer who had lived in Sevenoaks for a time) later had his own cycle shop in Otford.

Bat and Ball Junction, *c.* 1905

At the left of the picture is a pub called the Bat and Ball, which lent its name to this part of the town and to the town's first railway station, which opened in 1862. The Railway Tavern opened soon afterwards to capitalise on the commuter custom that the station brought to the area. Both pubs have now closed; the Bat and Ball's building is the only one of the two still standing.

Seal High Street, c. 1900

A village with Anglo-Saxon origins, Seal had its own market from at least the thirteenth century and two coaching inns. Historically an agricultural area, many of the village residents were employed on the Wildernesse estate on local farms. There are still a few shops in the village, but in recent years the two coaching inns have both closed, leaving The Five Bells, tucked away in Church Street, as the sole surviving pub.

Seal High Street, *c.* 1880
A very relaxed scene on what is nowadays a very busy bend on the A25 heading east out of Seal. The poster on the left-hand side advertises a demonstration, which will be attended by an MP, and another is for a National Fire Brigade's Union event in Tonbridge.

The Square, Riverhead, *c.* 1890
St Mary the Virgin is the parish church of Riverhead and Dunton Green. It was consecrated in 1831. The stone wall to the right marks the boundary of the Montreal Park estate.

The Dame School, Riverhead, *c.* 1890

To the right of St Mary's church was the Dame School. Run by the daughter of the stonemason whose yard was at the back of the building, children could be educated for two pennies a week. Following the building's demolition, a wooden memorial hall was built here that was replaced by the current hall in 1999.

The Square, Riverhead, 1950s

By the turn of the nineteenth century, Riverhead had around 300 residents, around half of whom lived in the village itself. In 1963, much of the centre of the village was swept away when the A25 was widened. Southbound traffic now passes where the houses on the right once stood.

London Road, Riverhead, 1900s

The fountain shown here was erected in 1897 to celebrate the Diamond Jubilee of Queen Victoria. It was paid for by public subscription. Originally sited at the junction of Maidstone Road and London Road, rising traffic volumes meant that it became a hazard to drivers so it was moved to the side of the road and later disposed of altogether during the widening of the A25 in 1963.

Wood's Garage, Riverhead, 1950s
Wood's garage and petrol station and all the buildings to its west up to The Square were lost during the widening of the A25.

The Parade, Riverhead.

The Parade, Riverhead, *c.* 1905

Of the buildings in this picture, only Heath's shop on the far right remains. It is now a restaurant. All of the other properties here were demolished as part of the modernisation of the centre of Riverhead and the A25 widening. The pub that stood on the western side of the road is remembered in the name of the row of shops with flats above: White Hart Parade.

London Road, Riverhead, 1900s

Looking west, this view shows in the distance some of the properties lost during the 1963 A25 widening. It also shows what a dominating position St Mary's church, with its coppered spire, occupies.

The Flemish House, London Road Riverhead, *c.* 1900

This unusual building was part of the tanyard, which extended to the opposite side of the road. It may have had Flemish origins, and certainly had a Continental appearance. The huge chimney was a particularly striking feature. It has since been replaced by housing.

London Road, Dunton Green, 1930s
The Red Line Tyre Mart and Garage occupied a large site on the south side of Longford Bridge. It later became a more modern petrol station, but the site now houses a bathroom store and a wine merchant.

Longford Bridge, Dunton Green, 1900s

The bridge pictured was built in 1636, as the River Darent flows here, and often rose quite high, flooding the road. The river ran past Longford Mill, which stands on the left, and it was used for swimming and boating.

Hamlin's Mill, Dunton Green, *c.* 1930s
The mill at Longford Bridge is likely to have had medieval origins and was was one of a number of mills along the course of the Darent. It closed down in 1947 but wasn't torn down until forty years later. The site is now a car dealership.

Dunton Green, *c.* 1900

Dunton Green was a centre of brick manufacture from the seventeenth century. The railway came here in 1868 when the main line running through Sevenoaks to London was opened, and in 1881 a branch line was opened linking Dunton Green to Brasted and Westerham. That line was closed in 1964.

Bessels Green, 1900s

The green here was originally part of a much larger area of common land. The building on the right of the photograph is Southdown House, the oldest surviving building on the green. It was originally the Red Lion Inn. The left-hand section of the terrace of cottages dates from the first half of the nineteenth century. Across the green, the Kings Head dates from at least 1686. The Unitarian Meeting House and Baptist church were built in 1716 and 1771 respectively.

Bessels Green, 1950s

This view shows the A25 at the eastern end of Bessels Green much more rural than it is now, before the M25 or the A21 Sevenoaks Bypass opened in 1967. The bypass was incorporated into the M25 in 1977.

Otford Parade, *c.* 1880

The farthest building in this nineteenth-century view is the village blacksmith's barn, and next to it is a seventeenth-century oak-framed house which was the blacksmith's home. This was later rebuilt and is now The Forge restaurant. The other houses have all become shops.

Otford, *c*. 1880

Otford is believed to derive its name from King Offa, who came to Kent in AD 775. Although the village grew considerably during the twentieth century, at its centre its structure remains little changed since this photograph was taken. The duck pond in the roundabout in the centre of the village has been Grade II listed since 1975, and is said to be the smallest listed structure in England.

Otford High Street, *c.* 1880

The closure of so many pubs in Sevenoaks (and indeed countrywide) over recent years makes it all the more surprising that Otford still has four. The Bull is at the right of the picture. It also has three churches: the medieval St Bartholomew's in the centre of the village, a Methodist church and an Evangelical Free church.

Chipstead, *c.* 1905
There had been a large house with its own estate in Chipstead for hundreds of years, and in the late seventeenth century a Palladian-style mansion, Chipstead Place, replaced the original house. Chipstead Place was demolished before the remainder of the estate was sold off for housing in 1964. Nearby, Chipstead Lake was formed as a result of gravel and sand excavation from the 1920s. The lake now extends to 61 acres and is home to a thriving sailing club.

'Donnington Manor', *c.* 1900

The Donnington Manor Hotel is not all it seems to be. In fact the cottage in the early photograph was converted into two farm cottages, and they stood on this site next to the old London Road in Dunton Green until the 1930s. Local builder Bill Newman then bought the land and set about building himself a large home using reclaimed materials. He gave his new home a name befitting a Tudor mansion: Donnington Manor. It is now a Best Western hotel.

D B L S ries 3808—Godden Green

Godden Green, *c.* 1905

A hamlet first settled in the sixteenth century, Godden Green, with its traditional pub and pond retains a quintessential English charm. The Bucks Head pub was built as a timber-framed house in the sixteenth century and a façade was added in the eighteenth century. The buck is the crest of the Sackville family of Knole. When this photograph was taken, many of the residents were employed by the Knole estate.

Sevenoaks Weald, the Prince of Wales, c. 1900s

Sevenoaks Weald lies just to the south of Sevenoaks, below the greensand ridge. The parish church, St George's, was built in 1821 as a 'chapel of ease' so that parishioners did not have to tackle the steep climb to Sevenoaks to worship at St Nicholas' church. The Prince of Wales pub shown here is nowadays Edwards Bar & Brasserie.

St Edith's Well, Kemsing, *c.* 1875

St Edith was the daughter of the Saxon King Edgar I. She was born in Kemsing in AD 961. This well was dedicated to St Edith, as it was believed that she gave the water healing properties. The waters were used to treat ailments into the twentieth century.

The White Rock, Underriver, 1900s

Deeds show that there were farming settlements in Underriver in the third century. A number of businesses were established in the hamlet of Great Underriver to meet the needs of the farming community. These included The White Rock, as well as a wheelwright's and a post office. The hamlet also had a school and a church.

Victoria Road, c. 1900

This is still a quiet residential road, just off London Road, between Lime Tree Walk and Argyle Road. However, like most other roads in the centre of the town, car parking can be a problem, something that the children in this photograph could surely never have imagined. Peacock's store on the left is now a private house.

Acknowledgements

I would particularly like to thank The Sevenoaks Society for giving me permission to use photographs from their extensive archive, which includes the collection of the late Gordon Anckorn, who did much to preserve Sevenoaks' early photographic history. I would also like to thank the photographers who took the original photographs. I have tried, as far as possible, to stand in their exact footsteps when taking many of my photographs, twenty-first-century traffic allowing.

Finally, I would like to thank my wife Louise and my sons Oliver and Nicholas for bearing with me while I was working on this book, and for much else besides.